Remotely Engaging
How to reach new audiences
by breaking out of the conference centre

Martin Shepherdly and Paul Cook

Who is this book for?

Chief Executives, Marketing and Communications Directors and Managers, Communications Managers, Conference Organisers working in or on behalf of associations or other membership bodies who appreciate that actively engaging with a higher proportion of their membership is essential if the organisation is to thrive.

Remotely Engaging

"Really clear and easy to follow. I encourage event planners the world over to read this straight talking, inspiring book and reach those audiences other events can't."

Marie-Claire Andrews – CEO, ShowGizmo Ltd

"Part of preparing for any event is in asking the right questions. Martin Shepherdly and Paul Cook cram a lot into a small space here, covering the big questions from working out the percentage of members you want to attend an event, through to positioning the lights correctly and how to choose and brief a presenter. Best of all, the authors' use of practical real-world examples demonstrates they are not armchair theorists - this is hard-won knowledge from the mouths industry professionals."

Nadine Dereza and **Ian Hawkins** – Co-Authors, Insider Secrets of Public Speaking

"This book is one of the most concise, easy to understand guides for anyone wanting to extend their reach to a remote audience and grow their attendance. You even might make your in-room experience better, too!"

Brandt Krueger – Event Technology Consulting

"Having held our own events with remote participants and speakers, this book is a great guide for associations wanting to extend the reach of their events. The easy to follow tips allow even a novice to get it right first time and avoid the pitfalls."

Mandy Torrens – Senior Exhibition Director, IBTM Global Events

Contents

Preface

A sad fact is that a large number of conference speakers aren't very engaging at all, even for the audience in front of them, never mind a remote audience viewing on their computers and mobile devices in another country and possibly even on a different day.

I don't just say this to be contentious; the assessment is based on my personal experience having been involved in the conference and events industry sector for some 37 years. This is not intended as a criticism of the game folk who are prepared to stand up and present their expert knowledge to an audience. It is an acknowledgement that being the greatest micro-biologist, the most adept legal brain or innovative technologist does not automatically mean you are going to be a great conference speaker. Just because you lead your field doesn't mean you are going to be a great communicator when you stand at the lectern and try to convey that expertise.

Of course with web broadcasting a conference there is a second remote audience to engage with, presenting further challenges to effective communication of ideas and knowledge and making it tougher still for the speaker.

For my first 25 years in this industry, part of my role as a conference producer was to help exactly these experts to give their best performance; to genuinely engage the audience in the room, in order to most effectively communicate their message. For the past 10 years or so, I have been involved with web broadcasting conferences and have come to understand the additional challenges and barriers to communication this presents. But I have also come to realise the opportunities it affords owners of conference content to create knowledge assets of lasting value. Opportunities, which to date are going largely unexploited.

To see what I mean, make a web search for "association conferences and congresses" and take a look at the event websites that show up. I guarantee that still, in 2016, only a small percentage of them offer any significant opportunity for remote participation, live or on demand. Most organisations are missing out on a substantial opportunity for return on the investment they are already making in creating their conferences.

For most associations, conferences are their biggest investment and they are throwing much of the latent value of their events away by NOT capturing the content. Often the incremental cost of doing so, pales into insignificance compared to the value of extending the reach of their event and the membership retention and acquisition capabilities that building a library of specialist knowledge makes possible.

Together with my colleague and co-author of this book, Paul Cook, we have successfully designed and produced numerous conferences that have broken out of the confines of the conference centre; that have extended the event's reach over distance and time to create valuable knowledge assets for the organising association or body. In so doing, we have learnt many lessons about what works and what doesn't work when it comes to capturing attention and actively engaging with a remote audience.

The purpose of this book is to condense that experience into a guide that will enable organisations to avoid some of the fundamental mistakes that are easily made when embarking on web broadcasting a conference or seminar. The intention is to help associations to shortcut the process of becoming *remotely engaging*, so that they too can unlock the full value of their conference content.

Martin Shepherdly, May 2016

The words we use

In exploring ways to break out of the conference centre to reach these new audiences, you will inevitably come across confusion-creating terminology. These terms have come about as essential frames of reference, as the technology we use has emerged and developed, over the last couple of decades. As the systems and technology we use are now becoming more established and accepted, we need to stop using some of the most misleading and unhelpful terms.

These terms tend to be used to describe three characteristics of an event; audience, format and delivery.

1.   The audience

Let's start with the most important ingredient in all of this, the audience. Terms most often heard to describe the differences between audiences are: *physical, virtual* and *hybrid.*

The use of the expressions physical and virtual when defining the audience is a particular bête noire for me. Of course no audience is virtual! The remote audience are just as real and physical as those sat in the room and, as stated in this book, they deserve equivalent attention.

Virtual events are computer generated, simulated events created by animators and featuring avatars and virtual worlds like Second Life[1]. There are companies out there offering *virtual exhibitions*, but to my

---

[1] http://secondlife.com/

mind, and whatever your opinion of their effectiveness, these have very little to do with the enhancement and extension of a conference or seminar, to an audience beyond the room.

The term *virtual event* is also sometimes used to describe an event that is delivered solely or primarily to a *virtual* (remote) audience. This adds further to the confusion.

The phrase *hybrid event* seemed to slip into common usage in the events industry a few years ago as a way to define an event extended to include a presence online. Despite my personal dislike of the word *hybrid* in this context – in my opinion it seems ugly and incongruous – at least it is not actually misleading! However, I contend that in time, all conferences and events of any merit are likely to have an online component and the additional noun will become redundant. They will all simply be events that have either a near or remote audience, or a combination of the two. I've summarised this in the table below.

CONFUSING AUDIENCE TERMS	PREFERRED AUDIENCE TERMS
Physical audience	**Near audience**
Virtual audience	**Remote audience**
Physical conference or event	
Virtual conference or event	**Conference or event** – it's just the make-up of the audience that changes
Hybrid conference or event	

2. Format

Webcasting and *webinars*; I have wrestled with and written about these terms on many occasions. The problem is that these made up words and others like them, are prejudiced by one's individual experience and can therefore mean completely different things to different people.

This is why, in the context of extending the reach of a conference, I prefer the term *web broadcasting,* or probably more accurately now, *web* and *mobile broadcasting*.

On the other hand, a *webinar* is specific to a purely remote audience and wouldn't normally be associated with a conference at all. To avoid confusion, the term is perhaps best reserved for standalone, online events, that use self-operated platforms such as Citrix's GoToWebinar and Adobe Connect. Sometimes you will hear the term *web conferencing* used to describe this kind of activity, which further adds to the confusion!

So, for the sake of clarity, throughout this book, we will be referring only to *web* and *mobile broadcasting*.

Everyone who listens to a radio, or watches television understands the concept of *broadcasting*. The *web* and *mobile* part simply defines the media we are using to transmit the broadcast; namely a combination of the internet and the 3G and 4G mobile networks.

All of which moves us neatly on, to how the web or mobile broadcast is actually delivered.

3. Delivery

Streaming refers to the process of delivering audio visual media (sometimes referred to as multimedia), that is continuously and concurrently received and consumed by the viewer or listener. (The term can apply to audio-only media as well as video with or without an audio track).

Before *streaming* developed, the only alternative was *file downloading;* a process by which the end-user obtained the entire file before watching or listening to it. The downside of *file downloading* for the viewer is the delay while it happens, as the entire file must be downloaded before it can be viewed. For the content owner, there was even greater negative impact, as once a file was downloaded, they had lost control of how that copy of the file was used.

In the early days of high speed broadband, *progressive downloading* became the rule. This allowed for the first part of the file to be viewed while the remainder progressively downloaded in the background. Watching the video all the way to the end without interruption, was dependent upon the broadband connection being fast and robust enough to allow the next part of the file to download in time. If the viewer caught up with the download, there would be a pause until the next part had downloaded and was ready to view.

These days, video encoding is much more efficient – so file sizes are smaller – and viewers are connecting at significantly higher speeds, meaning that *streaming* has become reliably smooth and is now ubiquitous.

Streaming comes in two varieties; *live* or *on demand*. There is little technical difference for the viewer – it really is the same difference as watching a live or pre-recorded programme on television. The significant differences are all at the presentation or delivery end.

Of course, *on-demand streaming* (sometimes also referred to as *video on demand* or *VOD*), as its name implies, is available at a time to suit the viewer. A *live stream* by definition takes place only at the time it is actually happening. It is not uncommon, for a live stream to be subsequently made available on-demand.

Remotely Engaging
How to reach new audiences
by breaking out of the conference centre

1. Why?

Before embarking on a lot of work to create a *remotely engaging* event, you need to fully explore the vital question of *strategy*.

Why are you doing this and what do you hope to achieve?

It is fundamentally important to give this question adequate consideration before getting wrapped up in the detail of delivery of the event.

Some event planners are just too quick to create their events and then later discover that they didn't achieve what they had hoped. Without a clear set of desired outcomes, it's not surprising that results are likely to disappoint.

In contrast the best *remotely engaging* events we come across are those where the association has clearly determined why the event exists, how they want it to affect their audience and the part the event plays in achieving the organisation's over-arching mission and core objectives.

Here are some ideas of really basic questions to ask, that may help to determine the "why" for your event. Of course these can apply to the physical event itself and need not be limited to the online component.

- How many members do you have in your association?

- Are your numbers growing or declining?

- Do you struggle to retain members?

- Do you have the right members?

- What proportion of your membership attend your events?

- Do your events attract non-members?

- Do delegates value your events?

- What are the long-term aims of your association?

- Are your local / regional / national / international / events helping your association fulfil key objectives?

Of course there will be many other questions you can ask that may be more relevant or specific to your organisation. Those above are merely intended to kick-start your thinking. You may choose to answer these questions by yourself or with your team. With some of them, it may be of even more value to ask your members and delegates. However you go about this, the insight and clarity that can come out of understanding *why* your events exist will help you determine clear objectives and make sure that you design future events that have the best chance of truly engaging all of your audiences.

Think about your events in new ways. Consider how you can reach new audiences by breaking out of the conference room and unlocking the full value of your event content. In turn, this will help you achieve those newly defined objectives.

If you need further inspiration to help you discover your answers to the whole question of "why?", take a look at the writings and videos of Simon Sinek at https://www.startwithwhy.com/

24

2. The rise of the remote audience

We have deliberately chosen to use the term *remote* to refer to the online audience in preference to the perhaps more commonly used adjective; *virtual*. This is because it helps to remind us that this particular audience is every bit as *real* as the physical audience in the room. From this point of view, they are certainly NOT virtual. To further level the playing field let's call the audience in the room, the *near* audience.

Starting off with something as basic as the language you use to refer to your audiences helps to begin to shift attitudes towards giving both audiences – *remote* and *near* – equal consideration, equal attention, equal importance.

It may be worth, at this point, briefly putting the rise in importance of this remote audience into some kind of commercial and technological context.

Of course we are all now electronically connected; "always on" if you like. But the increase in our connectedness has coincided with an ever increasing need to be more economic in our dealings, both financially and in terms of resources consumed. While we may not technically be in a recession, it often feels as if we are, as organisations are constantly being challenged to deliver a better return on investment. Budgets are relentlessly under pressure and time seems to be an ever more precious commodity.

So in an era when technology makes it easier for us to communicate remotely (that word again), traditional face-to-face events are under the profitability microscope and are having to stack up economically against ever more stringent measures.

Hence, from faltering steps in the early years of this century, the streaming or webcasting of events is now on the verge of becoming the norm. The reason is simply because creating an online presence for an event, allows us to involve a bigger, more widely located audience at a lower cost per head than a traditional event confined within the convention centre walls. Coinciding with this and for more or less similar reasons, it is not uncommon for physical attendances at established events to be decreasing.

It is the canny organisations that are embracing the rise of the remote audience as an opportunity, not to replace their face-to-face events, but rather to enhance them. There will always be a need for people to gather together on occasions; but not necessarily all of the people all of the time.

As delegates we need to become choosier about which events we physically attend and why, in order to ensure we personally get most value out of our investment of both time and the money we spend on attendance fees, travel and accommodation.

As organisers, we need to design events holistically to engage most effectively with our desired audience – near, remote or both – rather than blindly doing what we have always done.

For associations in particular, the rise of the remote audience presents an enormous and unprecedented opportunity to solve an age old problem that applies to so many of them. That problem, is how to actively engage with more than a small minority of their members. In the ten years or so that we have worked with associations I don't think I have ever come across one that ran conferences attended by the majority of their members. For most associations I have met, rather it is a tiny percentage of the membership that actively get involved.

Take as a case in point the Federation of Small Businesses in the UK. Now I'm not criticising the FSB at all – far from it as they are a prime example of an organisation that *is* taking active steps to engage with their remote audience. It just happens that they are a large association and it is relatively easy to find information about them. The member survey they published in 2013[2], states that at that time they had over 200,000 members. According to their website, their annual national conference in 2016 was attended by "over 1,100 attendees" which is approximately equivalent to 0.55% of their total membership.

Now for all I know, the FSB may not want their annual event audience to grow beyond 1,100 attendees and they do give members and non-members the opportunity to remotely engage through live streamed sessions and on demand recordings at http://www.fsblive.org/. They also run many regional and local events throughout the year.

And this is exactly what they should be doing. To not try and involve the

---

[2] http://www.fsb.org.uk/docs/default-source/fsb-org-uk/policy/assets/publications/fsb-member-survey-2013-uk.pdf

remaining 99.45% of their members in their annual conference – surely one of their biggest investments across the year – would be crazy indeed. Actively engaging members through this kind of activity is one way to help ensure members value what they get and make it more likely they will remain members. All power to the FSB who have clearly realised this.

Do the maths for your association. How many members do you have and what kind of percentage do you attract to your events? Is your audience in the minority? Can you use your events to more effectively engage with these non-attendees that may well make up the vast majority of your membership?

Like the FSB, if you run a large annual event, it is likely to be one of your biggest single investments of both money and resource. The opportunity is there to extend the reach and lifespan of that event and remotely engage with a broader range of members for a relatively small incremental outlay.

And, by the way, you can forget that myth about making your event available online cannibalising physical attendance; in reality what happens is that people joining online realise what they have been missing. Breaking out of the conference centre and opening up to a wider, remote audience can in itself be a great way to promote physical attendance at future events.

The fact is, people physically attend a conference for a whole series of reasons and the content of the conference sessions is not always top of that list. It's often got more to do with networking and career development, but sometimes the reasons can be as superficial as wanting a night away in a nice hotel or seeking the supposed glamour of international travel or even as prosaic as earning more hotel or airline loyalty points! So making the sessions available online certainly isn't going to stop these people.

On the flip side, you may have members who will not or cannot travel to the event no matter how enticing the fringe benefits. This might be for health or financial reasons or because they simply cannot afford the time out of the office. In some cases, they might not be able to get the requisite visas or are prohibited from travelling by their national government. Many of these people would value highly the opportunity to participate in the conference sessions without leaving home.

And then of course you can enhance the value for your *near* (physical) attendees too, by granting them access to the on demand content to view, revisit or share with colleagues upon their return home.

So this *rise of the remote audience* should be seen as a positive force that has created the biggest opportunity in recent years for event owners to increase the value of their events by engaging with a previously hard or impossible to reach audience. For some organisers, the *remote* audience may be significantly larger and potentially more valuable in helping achieve objectives than their traditional *near* audience!

3. A step up for sponsorship

Is your conference sponsor-able?

Sponsorship can be one of the most powerful ways for a company or brand to increase their exposure to a target audience. The great news for association event organisers, is that sector specific audiences are immensely attractive to sponsors. By definition, your precisely defined membership represents a pre-qualified audience for a company wishing to reach your particular industry or sector.

Having an event sponsor or sponsors doesn't work for everyone, but for the right associations they can be an effective way of raising credibility, profile and those all-important funds.

Do you attract sponsors for your events? If not, is it something you should consider? If you do, are you offering your sponsors the best possible opportunity to make their investment work?

Traditional event sponsorship models tend to revolve around branding and mentions of sponsor names in connection with one or more specific aspects of an event, or sometimes the event as a whole. While this can work well for some, the brand exposure achieved is often fairly transitory. Sponsorship of the name badge, a drinks reception or a lunch, positions the sponsors name and brand passively in front of people. Sometimes there might be the opportunity for a representative to address the audience, but rarely is there much further explanation of the sponsor's offer or exploitation of the occasion that can have much lasting impact.

This is why the smart associations are now having a lot of success selling sponsorship of their online conference content.

Putting your conference sessions online; in other words, taking the presentations out of the confines of the congress centre and making the knowledge available after the event (sometimes for a considerable period of time) enables the creation of sponsorship opportunities of significantly greater value and duration than the packages to which sponsors have all become accustomed. And it's always good to have something fresh and new to offer sponsors.

This medium is ideally suited to sponsorship. It might be simply a case of adding the sponsor's brand or message to the content viewing page, or it could be included on registration and log in pages, registration confirmation emails and so on.

But where you can offer even higher value sponsorship packages is with the injection of sponsor video content into the live or on demand stream. The form this might take can vary from a simple logo 'sting' that plays before each presentation, to a video commercial that intersperses recordings much like a TV ad break, to specially commissioned sponsored programme content that sits alongside the session recordings.

So how does this mark a step up for sponsorship? Well, quite simply because you can offer packages that have much greater potential impact and longevity – and therefore value – for the sponsor.

Now, you can offer something to sponsors that will last longer than the duration of the event.

Now, sponsors have the added value of reaching a much wider and larger audience than just the near delegates.

Now, sponsors have the opportunity to be strongly associated with education, knowledge and thought leadership in your specific subject area over a significant period of time.

Of course the first hurdle is to find your ideal sponsor partner. For some associations that partner may be obvious and already known to you, but for others it is no easy task to find the ideal sponsor. Fortunately, there are a number of agencies and matching platforms emerging to help bring sponsors and content owners together[3].

If you decide to embark on a search for a sponsor, always remember that no matter how worthy your mission or cause, sponsorship is not a right. To be successful you will have to demonstrate to a potential partner that sponsoring your content will deliver value back to the sponsoring organisation. It will be paramount to them, that they achieve a return on their investment (however they measure it) and you will need to keep this front of mind when approaching and negotiating with a potential sponsor.

---

[3] Here are two sponsor matching sites that you might want to take a look at
http://www.sponsormonster.co.uk/
https://www.sponsormyevent.com/

Sponsorship is at its most effective, when a symbiotic relationship is established between sponsor and content owner that can continue over multiple events. But it is a relationship that will need careful nurturing if it is to be sustained.

4. Reach out for more

No longer restricted by the physical constraints of the venue and with the ability to extend the life of your content beyond the few days of the conference, you have an opportunity to increase the impact of your events exponentially!

By taking the step to reach out to a remote audience, not only will you broaden your opportunity to engage with more of your target audience or membership, but you will also create the potential to generate more revenue.

There are any number of innovations you can explore once you decide to take the step to engage with a remote audience. We have already touched on the sponsorship opportunity, but income can often be derived from simply selling access to live streams and recordings.

For many organisations, this can prove to be very lucrative, particularly when the subject matter is in high demand. However, to be successful, extensive marketing to the target audience is required – especially in the early days.

I have been amazed in the past at how naïve people can be in this regard. One association client, who shall remain nameless of course, once complained to me strongly about the lack of sales of their conference recordings. Upon further investigation, it turned out they had simply posted a link to the recorded content on a page buried deep in their website and then just waited, expecting people to find it. To make matters worse, when we looked at their website analytics, it turned out that traffic on the site was pitifully low anyway. Not only did they need to put some marketing effort behind their content recordings, but they also needed to reassess their whole online strategy, as plainly the website was not offering what members wanted or needed.

If you do decide to venture into selling your content always remember this... **if you are offering content of genuine value to your audience, they will be prepared to pay for it.** If they are not prepared to pay, then you are not offering them content that they want or value. It's a bit like the clichéd (but none the less true) marketing mantra that to be successful you must "Sell what the customer needs, not what you want to sell." However, the marketing and operational side of creating paid-for online content is a big subject in its own right and it is beyond the scope of this book to deal with this in any detail.

Another way we have seen many organisations get more bang for their buck, is by allowing the creation of "hub events". These are effectively breakout conferences, held around the country or around the globe, where people gather together for a more shared experience. Often they will join together to participate in the live streamed sessions and during the meal and refreshment breaks, hub event participants have their own time to network, discuss and explore issues raised during the sessions, in the same way as the near audience in the main conference centre.

A commercial model we have seen applied successfully is to sell the rights to a local organiser to create a hub event. The local organisers then cover their costs and potentially make a profit by selling tickets to attend their hub event.

Advertising is another potential source of revenue. If you are using YouTube, you can of course simply set up your channel to be monetized through YouTube ads. You could also consider adding Google Ads to your viewing pages. Others sell video ads which can be inserted into the stream pre- mid- or post-roll.

Once you have captured your content there are many other ways to exploit it for gain for the organisation. I use the word gain as opposed to *profit* as it is not always necessarily about cash. For many associations, especially those that create educational content, the value is as much in being able to disseminate knowledge in their specific subject. For at least one of our association clients this is their core purpose. For any association that needs to educate or advise their members, creating a library of valuable educational assets can play a vital role in retaining members and recruiting new ones.

The Bill Gates mantra that "content is king" may have become an overused saying, but when it comes to internet video content specifically, no one can argue that it isn't growing in consumption and by an ever increasing audience. In June 2016[4], Cisco released their VNI Global IP Traffic Forecast, 2015-2020.

---

[4] http://www.cisco.com/c/en/us/solutions/service-provider/visual-networking-index-vni/index.html#~overview

Remotely Engaging

This highlighted the following projections;

- By 2020, there will be nearly 4.1 billion global Internet users, up from 3.0 billion in 2015 and representing more than 52 percent of the world's population.

- By 2020, there will be 26.3 billion networked devices and connections globally, up from 16.3 billion in 2015. (That's more than 3.5 devices per person!)

- Globally, the average fixed broadband connection speed will increase 1.9-fold, from 24.7 Mbps in 2015 to 47.7 Mbps by 2020.

- Globally, IP video will represent 82 percent of all traffic by 2020, up from 70 percent in 2015.

The obvious conclusion one draws from these mind boggling statistics is that there is clearly a vast market and an enormous appetite for video content. So event owners that are already creating educational content for their conferences, seminars and events – often at significant expense in time, money and resources – owe it to themselves to unlock the hidden value of that content by giving it a life beyond the single occasion and place of their conference.

Content itself may not necessarily be king, but the owners of that content have the opportunity to rule over their particular subject domain.

5. Now you have <u>two</u> audiences

It is becoming more and more common for associations to webcast their events and, in turn, increasingly important for them to transform their remote delegates into remote participants rather than merely passive viewers. In this way, it becomes a much more participative experience than just sitting and watching a video and therefore ultimately more likely to be effective and achieve your objectives.

So, all of a sudden you now have two very different audiences. But before we get on to talking about their different needs, there are some basic considerations you need to give to venue selection right up front.

Now, we are not here to tell event planners how to do their job in terms of selecting suitable venues, but there are three basic technical considerations that need to be taken into account and they can be fundamental to a live stream happening at all!

1. Connectivity

   To live stream an event requires high speed internet access. This may sound a ridiculously obvious a statement, but unfortunately experience has shown that it is not always in the forefront of the mind of the venue booker! However, just because a venue may not be able to provide a permanent broadband connection doesn't necessarily preclude it from being suitable. Alternative solutions such as a portable satellite set up or a bonded 4G service can often be installed. While being an additional cost, these services are considerably more affordable than they used to be, and can make a venue, ideal in every other aspect, viable.

Remember, if you need Wi-Fi access in the room for near delegates, this will be an additional load on the connectivity and should use a completely separate service to that used for live streaming.

2. Camera view

    There needs to be a suitable camera position or positions, where they can get line of sight to the lectern, stage or wherever the action is taking place, high enough to avoid being interrupted by delegate heads and clear of low hung chandeliers! Look for any columns that may interrupt the view as well. Think about the background and if a set is being installed then make your designer aware you will be capturing it on camera. If, instead, it is just the walls of the room, consider how that will look. Clean and simple is best. At all costs avoid having the action take place against a window, where the daylight backlight will mean the speakers will just appear in silhouette.

3. Sound and lighting

    It is a false economy not to engage a professional to provide the sound equipment. Good sound is vital to success.

    On many occasions we are forced to work with the normal room lighting, which can be sufficient, but you will get a far superior result if you install a proper rig to light the presentation area or stage.

So, now back to those two audiences...

Whether you are streaming your event live or making it available on demand, you now have two very different audiences to please and you need to give them equal precedence; you need to give them equal consideration. They have different needs, objectives, distractions and attention spans and you must keep that integral to your thinking when planning your events.

To be successful you must first of all do your "homework". Here are a few things to keep in mind.

First of all, you need to know both your audiences; near and remote. Specifically, for the remote audience, consider...

- How are they going to be accessing the stream?

- What kind of technical limitations are they going to have?

- What kind of devices are they going to be using?

- Do they have experience of accessing online content?

- How tech-savvy are they?

All these things and more need to be taken into account.

This will help you determine what technology solution is right for your event and for your delegates.

Whatever you do, keep the solution simple. Sometimes it may be worth allowing remote delegates the opportunity to try it out in advance, so that when the event takes place they are already familiar with the interface. We have seen events that have poor audience take up because it all looks just too complex. Similarly, try and avoid solutions that require participants to download software or apps. This can become an obstacle with some delegates who don't want (or in some IT environments may not be permitted) to download additional software. This is especially true if it uses up precious space on their device and may only be relevant for the duration of the event.

Try and find ways to engage with your remote audience prior to the conference. This can be an invaluable way of building anticipation and creating a social media buzz that will help encourage others to join. Think about how you can continue this engagement after the conference itself through continued discussion and access to on demand content.

You also need to consider what time zones the audiences are living in? If the near audience and remote audience are in the same time zone, then clearly the business of planning the schedule at least is straightforward.

If your event straddles more than one time zone, then scheduling the programme becomes altogether more complex. Within and near Europe you can be dealing with time differences of between one and four hours, but if you have a global audience you could quite possibly have remote delegates where the differential is more than twenty hours. In this case you need to give very careful thought to structuring your programme, possibly considering repeat broadcasts or alternative schedules depending upon where key audiences are located.

This planning has to relate back to the original objectives of your event and that vital knowledge of your audiences. There would be little point in scheduling to accommodate a specific time zone, when in the bigger scheme of things, it is just not important to the overall success of your event. Similarly, if an audience in a particular time zone are vital to success, then consider building the programme around a schedule suited to their convenience.

Remember also to look out for daylight saving time changes that happen across the globe. Not everywhere changes on the same date which can be very confusing if your event coincides with a change.[5]

Be clear about start and finish times and stick to them. Conferences are notorious for starting late and over or under running. I would argue this is very bad form in any circumstance, but when you have a remote audience this is simply not acceptable. Make sure everyone – technical crew, venue staff, speakers, delegates, sponsors – all understand the importance of this from the outset.

In addition to the question of time zones you also need to take into account major religious and national holidays.

As part of "knowing your audience" it is useful to be aware of faiths and nationalities. If you decide to hold your event close to a major religious

---

[5] This is a very useful site when scheduling an event that crosses time zones and even has an international meeting planner application http://www.timeanddate.com/worldclock/meeting.html

holiday, then you could be jeopardising the attendance of a whole section of your audience. Check out the key dates and work around them.[6]

And don't forget that the working week is not necessarily Monday – Friday. In many Muslim countries the normal working week is traditionally Sunday to Thursday.

And you can apply the same thinking to avoiding clashes with major events that take place on a regular basis, be it annually, bi-annually or another frequency. These might be specific to your sector or of broader interest. Work around these dates to maximize your opportunity of getting the audience you want for your remotely engaging event.

Language is something else that should not be overlooked. We, in the English speaking world, can be particularly lazy and inconsiderate with regard to this!

When your event is being streamed across the globe it is vital to know what languages your delegates understand. If an assumption is made that whatever language or languages the meeting is conducted in will be widely understood, and it isn't, then you will encounter problems and have upset delegates to deal with.

You must ensure all your speakers are briefed to consider that English (or the language of the meeting) may not be the audience's first language and they should moderate their speech accordingly, so that all

---

[6] Once again, the Time and Date site has useful information regarding national and religious holidays http://www.timeanddate.com/holidays/

have the best chance of understanding.

In some cases, it may be appropriate to add simultaneous translation or subtitles. This does add a layer of complexity and cost, but if you represent a multi-national, multi-lingual association, this can be vital to ensure you remotely engage your delegates.

And you need to remind delegates – both near and remote – that they are equally important. Let them know that your event will include both near and remote delegates. If the near delegates understand and appreciate that there are remote participants, you will have a better chance of achieving your goals.

In terms of general behaviour, your near delegates need to be aware that they are being recorded and may be heard and seen by people outside the room. When conducting a Q & A, in a small conference room, it is not unusual for delegates to be too impatient to wait for a microphone to arrive before asking their question. If they understand that the remote delegates simply won't hear their question, they may be a little less hasty to speak. Just by making this small element a part of your modus operandi, you will create a far better overall experience for everyone.

Try and find ways that both sets of delegates are able to interact with each other. Making it possible for them to connect will have benefits for you and them. We deal with interactivity and some techniques that can be deployed in more detail later in this book.

Once you have done your homework and know your audiences you are in a position to set about designing your event. We use the term *design* intentionally: actively *design* your event; don't just let it happen!

Even more important, if your event has happened previously, such as in the case of an annual congress, don't just do what you've always done! Now you have two audiences you need to do things differently. The most successful remotely engaging events are those where every detail is considered, designed and implemented, always with the best experience for the audience in mind.

But one final plea when considering your two audiences; whatever you do, don't forget to add an element of "show time"! It is many times more difficult to capture the attention of an audience remotely than it is in the room. To give you the best chance, you need to think about *production values*. This phrase is often bandied around and not always understood. It refers to the quality of the camera work as well as the lighting, sound and scenery used to improve the viewing experience. In my view it should also include non-technical aspects such as the way you structure your content. You need changes of pace. some light and shade, the occasional injection of appropriate humour or even drama.

As a general principal, if you have got the technical part of this right, remote participants will rarely notice or comment, because it is a comfortable experience. Get it wrong and they are likely to let you know straight away. The poor sound quality or insufficient lighting, or whatever the problem is will become a huge distraction and people will literally switch off.

High quality video and sound are essential and getting the lighting and backdrop right will help to provide a bit of polish and pizazz. But to truly engage people there has to be an element of entertainment amongst the information and education.

6. From passive to active

When it comes to remotely engaging events, there is no one size that fits all. The question that you constantly need to answer throughout the design and production of your event is: *What am I seeking to achieve?*

Perhaps you want your delegates to do something differently as a result of your event? Perhaps you just need to impart some knowledge or a new technique. Understanding what outcomes you want will naturally lead you to being able to create your programme.

Whether you decide to apply some or all of the techniques referred to in this book, or others we don't cover, to actively engage your remote audience you need to be very clear on your objectives from the outset. This is true of course in regard to your near (physical) audience, but it becomes many times more important when you have a remote audience.

At the risk of being repetitive, be 100% clear on why you are doing this; why you are trying to engage with your audience and what you are hoping to achieve.

All events with a remote audience have their place on the scale that ranges from *very passive* to *very active*. Where your event *should* sit on that scale depends entirely on what you are trying to achieve. Where it *actually* sits will be a guide to how successful you have been in achieving your objectives!

A *very passive* event would be one where the remote delegates simply view a live (or more likely on demand) video.

A slightly less passive event would give remote participants the opportunity to submit one or two questions via Twitter or a web form.

At the other end of the scale, a *very active* event would involve remote delegates in a multitude of activities that, along with viewing a (most likely) live video stream could include;

- Submitting questions and comments

- Contributing via social media

- Taking part in polls or voting

- Taking part in games or competitions

- Taking part in surveys or tests

- Contributing via audio or video link

- Free downloads

There is no point in rushing off to create a very active event unless it will help to meet your objectives. You can create a lot of activity and noise but if it doesn't lead to furthering the objectives of the event then you could have saved a lot of effort and settled for a more passive approach.

And you can purposefully encourage activity and increased engagement through incentives. A lot of associations now allow members to earn CPD/CME credits by attending their online events.

There are all sorts of techniques you can apply, that not only encourage people to participate more, but also provide you with a delegate feedback loop. From this, you might be able to get an indication of how long people are watching, how long they are staying engaged with the event, how are they acting and feeling as a result of their participation. The exact nature of the incentives that will be appropriate will be different for each association and event, but this can be an important area to focus on as it can help ensure a measurable return on investment.

One thing is consistent, irrespective of the level of activity; remote delegates require their own programme. Of course this can be derived from and worked around the onsite programme, but the design needs to be carefully considered with the remote delegate in mind.

We have seen it happen all too often that barely any attention is paid to the remote delegates when the programme is constructed. It quickly becomes obvious to them that they have been forgotten and they simply switch off. Either intellectually and possibly temporarily, by getting distracted by email, web surfing or something else going on around them, or physically and permanently by shutting the viewing page down!

By way of an example (I'm glad to say this was several years ago), I witnessed the chair of very large conference at London's Royal Albert Hall who started proceedings by saying how delighted he was that the audience in the room was being joined by many thousands of viewers online and what an exciting addition this was to the event. A reasonable start, but that was the last acknowledgement or reference to the remote audience that was made over the entire duration of the event. On our control panel we watched the number of viewers dwindle away as they one by one disengaged from the event which had completely failed to engage them.

Ensuring the design of the event is right for your remote delegates requires just as much care and attention as putting together the near (onsite) delegate programme.

Again, every scenario will be different, but here are some starter questions for you to consider in making sure that your remote delegates are engaged with your event;

- How will remote delegates view and interact with the event?
- Will they be able to submit comments or questions? If so how?
- Is there adequate communication of all the things they need to know to be able to make the most of the event? The easier you make it for your remote delegates the better their experience will be and the more chance you will achieve your objectives.
- Have you shown the remote delegates how they can interact with your event?
- What are the communications channels?
- Who should they contact if they experience technical difficulties?
- How will you accommodate and communicate late programme changes?
- Is it easy to see what is happening when, so the remote delegate can organise their day?

- What happens during conference breaks?

And for the larger congress type events;

- What strategy are you going to employ with multiple breakout streams? Will some of these be streamed live or just be made available on demand?

Put yourself in the remote delegate's seat and imagine the day progressing. Follow the event path from start to finish and you can be sure to close any gaps in your planning.

But be careful not to go too far the other way and ram continuous and unrelenting content at the remote participant!

Yes, there are many things you can offer while the near delegates are having a break including interviews, polls, chats, games and all sorts of other activities. But ask yourself; are you giving your remote delegates enough time for eating, drinking, comfort breaks and reflection on preceding sessions?

Are you providing enough breaks so they can grab a coffee and check their email and messages? Because if you don't, they will skip sessions in order to take care of these things.

There is nothing wrong with, for example, studio interviews with speakers following their presentations, but please ensure that you have allowed your remote delegates some downtime in their programme in the same way that there will be breaks for near delegates.

With a carefully planned programme providing a balance of rich content with adequate breaks and time to reflect, your remote delegates will be much more likely to become fully engaged and stay the course throughout the event.

7. Interactivity

Here are some really practical ways that you can remotely engage with your audience.

The most obvious way to engage your remote participants is through interactivity. But there are a number of different levels of complexity and sophistication, with which you can interactively engage people.

At the simplest level this can be a text based method where delegates can ask a question just by typing into a text box placed on the viewing page and pressing "send". The submitted questions then appear on a closed page being monitored in the conference room. Here a suitable person, and they might be on- or off-stage, is assigned to select questions and have them asked in the room. In this scenario, no other delegates can see what others are asking, so it is a *closed question* model. This is very straightforward for both the organiser and the participants to use.

Moving up a level from that is moderated interactivity. There is a tool that we use to do this called CoveritLive[7].

This is an affordable application that is easy to use and allows for moderation of comments either posted directly on the webcast page or via social media platforms. Effectively, CoveritLive allows you to 'harvest' Twitter, Instagram, Facebook and even YouTube posts using specific hashtags and search terms and an invited moderator or team of

---

[7] CoveritLive http://www.coveritlive.com/

moderators can publish the selected posts on the viewing page. As this is all conducted through a web browser, the moderators can be anywhere in the world – all they need is a computer or tablet and an internet connection. Unlike the closed question model, all viewers can see the published comments and questions.

Our good friends and long term clients The International Society for Ultrasound in Obstetrics and Gynaecology (ISUOG) have used this approach on many live webcasts with us. Their Event Manager Lorraine Reese, when talking about her experience of using CoveritLive to engage with remote delegates, said;

"For us it has been really useful, in an event we did last month we had 18 questions from our 'live-streamers' [remote delegates] which was more than triple the number of questions we got from inside the room! Every time a speaker went on stage, my colleague who was moderating the live stream was able to link directly to information we had on that speaker, either other lectures, or articles they have produced in the journal, thereby directing our online participants back to our website.

And we also noticed they [remote delegates] created their own little community. So if someone asked a question, someone else watching the live stream answered it, rather than waiting for the speakers to answer it themselves. So, we loved it! It was super-easy, really intuitive."

CoveritLive is just one example of a tool that is available at very low cost that can readily be integrated into your web cast events to aid interactivity. And you can extend it further into polling.

Polling is another way of engaging people; rather than waiting for them to ask questions, you can ask a question of your audience.

One of the downsides of using a polling solution on the web viewing page, is that your responses will be from your remote audience only and it excludes the near audience. Increasingly of course, for larger events at least, an event app can provide a polling facility. Of course then you have the reverse problem as remote delegates are unlikely to be persuaded to download the event app and now it is they who will be excluded from polls. If you don't have the benefit of a suitable event app or you simply want to avoid the disparity between remote and near delegates, then we strongly recommend you consider Poll Everywhere[8].

Poll Everywhere enables the integration of polling directly in the speakers' PowerPoint presentations, both to display questions and to show live responses. Anyone can respond using a mobile phone, Twitter, or a web browser, so using this will give much more meaningful results as you are allowing your remote delegates and your in-the-room-audience to participate on an equal basis.

There are of course many other such apps available and more being created all the time. We include these two examples here to stimulate your thinking in terms of ways that you can interactively engage your

---

[8] Poll Everywhere https://www.polleverywhere.com/

audiences without investing a fortune.

The third level of interactivity is where contributions by audio and video from speakers in remote locations are included in the event. Of course any organisation that has a video conference suite in their offices will be familiar with this concept. However, even if your association has invested in such technology, it is rarely portable and is unlikely to be something you can readily access in the context of a conference. This is where "software video conferencing" comes into play.

By using software products[9] such as Oovoo, Skype and Zoom, you can enable multiple remote presenters and panellists to present to your physical and remote audiences and have them involved as seamlessly as your presenters in the room.

This can be taken to different levels of complexity. Recently, we conducted a live webcast in the UK for the Information Commissioner's Office (ICO), who were holding a conference in Cheshire on the subject of enforcement. They wanted two leading industry players, who weren't able to take the time out of their diaries to travel to the UK, to nonetheless be able to join in the panel discussion sessions. One was in Washington DC and the other in Hong Kong. We connected the two remote speakers into the conference room at the appropriate time using Zoom. Appearing, for the audience in the room, on large screens either side of the panel desk, they could be seen and heard as well as

---

[9] Oovoo https://www.oovoo.com/
Skype https://www.skype.com/
Zoom https://zoom.us/

the physically present panellists. The online audience received the video and audio of whoever was talking at any one moment, irrespective of whether that speaker was in Cheshire, Washington or Hong Kong.

This was a relatively straightforward use of software video conferencing. Somewhat more complex was an event we live streamed a few years ago from Abu Dhabi in the UAE. On that occasion, over a two-day conference, there were eleven speakers, only two of whom were physically present in Abu Dhabi. The other nine were distributed literally worldwide – from Auckland to Vancouver!

And of course you can get much more complex than that, when you start to introduce "hub events" with local breakout sessions.

A very good example of this was Intercommunity 2015[10], the Internet Society event which had attendees from more than 141 countries and 15 hubs. The Internet Society billed it as "a global meeting of the Internet Society, on the Internet, for the Internet

And the complexity levels can be pushed for as far as you have an appetite! The only real limit is your ability to plan, prepare and test and then having the available resources to deliver on the day.

---

[10] https://www.internetsociety.org/intercommunity2015/

8. Gamification

One of the most often heard buzzwords around the conference and events industry in recent years is *gamification.*

Ugly made-up marketing term it may be, but its profligate use and the fact that there doesn't seem to be an alternative term means that a book on the subject of remotely engaging an audience wouldn't be complete without its mention.

This subject follows on the theme of the previous chapter as *gamification* is all about interaction. Like many made up words, people have different ideas as to its meaning, but the main concept is that game components are included within the design of the event.

The Oxford Dictionary defines *gamification* as:

The application of typical elements of game playing (e.g. point scoring, competition with others, rules of play) to other areas of activity, typically as an online marketing technique to encourage engagement with a product or service

Of course in our context that "product or service" is the conference or event.

If you think that games have no place in conferences and events, then you may be missing out on an opportunity to secure more active engagement of your participants. With the proliferation of smart mobile devices has come an unprecedented appetite for games or apps with aspects of *gamification*. Throw into the mix augmented reality (AR) and you have the building blocks for some truly creative developments in audience engagement. This is yet to become mainstream in the conference world, but I believe it will not be long before it is.

And if you think games are just for kids, then bear in mind that in July 2016, the wildly successful Pokémon Go had a user base of 44% millennials[11] (18-34 age group).

The challenge with incorporating aspects of *gamification* within an event is to ensure that the game component or components support the overall objectives you have identified for your event. (I refer you back to Chapter 1.) If the game element helps to achieve or exceed the objectives you have set then great. If not, it may become a costly distraction for both the organising team and the participants.

Used well, *gamification* can be a powerful way of helping your delegates interact whether they are near or remote.

This whole area is only really beginning to emerge as a component of conferences and we can expect some rapid developments over the next couple of years, both technologically and creatively.

---

[11] https://intelligence.slice.com/pokemon-go-caught-em/

In the meantime, here are some basic aspects of *gamification* to consider for your specific event:

- Leader boards can work particularly well and can certainly encourage the more competitive people to become more engaged. But, beware of cultural differences when encouraging competition, as the inclination to compete can vary dramatically.

- Social media mentions, photographic competitions and quizzes are just three techniques you can use to incorporate gaming elements into your event. But, whatever you decide to do, just remember that you have two audiences to include in your thinking.

- Decide whether a team or individual game will best serve your objectives. If team based, how will the teams be selected and organised? How will this be different for near and remote audiences?

- And don't forget the technology that a delegate will need in order to participate. As I said in Chapter 5, you need to know your audience, and that includes knowing what devices they use. Tailor your activity accordingly. You don't want disgruntled delegates who couldn't take part because they didn't have a smartphone or tablet.

9. Remote presenters

Having carefully deliberated over and meticulously designed your event programme, consider this scenario.

It becomes apparent that one or more of your ideal presenters are located in different countries or even continents to that where your event is taking place. Clearly, this means someone – normally the event organiser, or sometimes a sponsor – is going to incur travel and accommodation expenses on behalf of the presenter. It also means the presenter is going to have to be prepared to sustain disruption to their schedule and invest a significant amount of time, relative to the actual duration of their presentation, to travel to and from the event.

Now that's all fine if the organiser's budget permits and the presenter is willing and available. But it doesn't always work that way. So, what happens if you don't have the funds to pay the additional logistical costs? What if the presenter in question is keen to speak, but less enthusiastic or able to dedicate the time required for travelling? What can you do?

In a second scenario, you might have made a conscious decision not to bring in speakers located any significant distance from the venue. Something not uncommon in this environmentally and budget sensitive era. Does this mean you have to limit your choice of presenters to those who happen to be nearby?

Well fortunately, no. We now have the technology to allow a speaker to present remotely, using a standard broadband connection and with equipment they may well already possess or can access at very low cost.

Including remote presenters as part of your programme can be exciting and challenging in equal measure and often both at the same time!

Once again, success is dependent upon adequate preparation. Any remote presenters need to be carefully and comprehensively briefed as to how the event will unfold and what is expected of them.

With remote presenters you need to allow plenty of time for preparation, testing and rehearsal well in advance of the event itself. Clearly communicate this to them in advance and provide them with a schedule as well as technical support and guidance.

Of course you will also need to think about any additional audio visual support you will need at the conference location, in order to ensure your remote presenters can be seen and heard by near delegates and injected into the live stream for the remote audience.

If you have a number of remote presenters, consider producing a handbook or briefing pack that covers things like:

The computer specification they will need and any software they will need to install

- The computer doesn't need to be particularly high-end; a good current machine will suffice.
- Software to be installed will vary depending on exactly how your

event is being managed.

- It's important to make sure they turn off any programs running in the background which will not only drain resources but may pop up messages or warnings without notice that could interrupt your webcast.

Required internet connection speed

- The higher speed and more robust the connection the better the quality and reliability.
- If the speaker is presenting from a workplace, make sure to engage the help and support of the in-house IT team.

The importance of finding a quiet location

- "Noises off" are distracting and disruptive for presenter and viewer alike.
- Avoid a location near a corridor or other thoroughfare. This may be silent when you are testing but suddenly inundated with chatter and door slamming when the actual event takes place.
- Make sure all telephones in the room are turned off or muted.

Audio and video equipment they will need

- Internal webcams fitted to laptop computers can be okay quality but are not great in terms of getting a good angle of view to the presenter's face. Far better to have a separate camera on a tripod. This might simply be an HD webcam or may involve a professional camera and operator. It all depends on your attitude to quality and your available budget.

- The same applies to microphones. Laptop on board mics are less than ideal as they will pick up all the noises in the room and in particular the sounds of the presenter tapping their keyboard, if they are running their own slides, as well as any shuffling of papers or squeaky chairs. Far better to invest in a separate condenser microphone, either on a stand or that can be clipped to the speakers clothes, close to their mouth.

Principles of good lighting

- Good lighting is almost an art form that can take years of experience to do well, but the basic principles are simple. You need the brightest part of the picture to be the presenters face and the background to be relatively darker.
- Sometimes the existing available light is sufficient, but often results can be hugely enhanced by the addition of a couple of well-placed lamps. Again decisions in this regard are likely to be budget-driven, but sourcing a couple of LED panels on stands need not be expensive and can make the world of difference to the quality of the image you achieve.
- At all costs avid the subject being set against a window during daylight hours – you will never be able to compensate for the backlight of the sun.
- Try not to rely on daylight, as the light can vary so much in a short space of time as clouds come and go.

What not to wear

- In the past video struggled to resolve certain colours and patterns, so this was a much more important consideration than it is now. The most important thing in these high-definition days is to avoid too much contrast, particularly taking into account the subject's skin tone. If clothing is vividly contrasting the camera will struggle to balance the exposure correctly for the face. So, dark-skinned people should avoid wearing white or very light colours, whereas the pale-skinned should avoid black or very dark clothing.

The importance of a tidy background

- Clutter or movement in the background is a huge distraction for the viewer.

How to show their presentation slides

- If the presenter is running their slides themselves, make sure they are familiar with the software they are using and have rehearsed the process of showing their slides a number of times.

How Q&A sessions will be handled

- There are many ways of doing this. The vital thing is that whatever method is being used, you inform the presenter of the process in advance, so they are not caught out.

Tips for presentation style when presenting remotely

- Presenting effectively to a camera while imagining the audience watching in the conference room hundreds of miles away is not an easy skill to acquire and one that only tends to come with practice.

- The advice you give will largely depend upon the context within which the speaker is appearing, but perhaps the single most valuable piece of advice you can offer is to ask them to try and behave exactly as they would if they were actually sat or standing on stage in the room. They need to be just as animated and work just as hard at getting their messages across as if they were physically presenting to the audience.

Insist on testing that they have all this in place a couple of weeks before the event, by having a dry run with them. Make sure that as far as possible they use the same location and set up as they are planning to use on the day.

Next, conduct a full dress rehearsal with them. The smart thing to do is to record this rehearsal, so that should there be any technical or logistical issues on the day, you can always 'play in' the recording.

If a remote presenter isn't able to handle the technology and can't source any help locally, or is unwilling to devote the time to testing and rehearsing, then you perhaps need to reconsider their place on the agenda. If you don't, and the worst happens, you may be left with a gaping hole in your programme.

The important thing is that there is plenty of communication with the remote presenters to identify and eliminate problems well in advance of going live. It is in everyone's interest to keep them informed every step of the way.

Plan.

Communicate.

Test.

Communicate.

Rehearse.

Communicate.

If you do all this, then there is every reason to expect a smooth running and engaging event with your remote presenters making a major contribution.

10. The host

Creating additional content specifically for your remote audience is another way to keep remote delegates engaged.

A good approach to apply here is that taken by many reality TV shows that provide a recap after each ad break as well as a preview before the next. This allows people to dip in and out more easily and still know what is going on. It is a very good way to keep those remote delegates engaged, because unlike most of the delegates in the room, they are less likely to join the entire proceedings. As long as they are well informed about the programme they can cherry pick the sessions that are of real interest to them.

Clearly doing this will require someone to fulfil the role of presenter. But if you are going to go down this route, the presenter selected should be capable of doing a lot more than just a recap and preview. Chosen well and directed wisely, they can contribute much more to the success of the event than that. Think of the role as that of a TV style anchor-man. Now I don't suggest you rush off and find your very own Ron Burgundy, but ideally this would be a professional presenter. I have known a number of associations that have been able to find capable in-house talent to carry out this function, but they are quite rare and it is a lot of pressure to put on someone, so do make sure they are genuinely up to the task.

Let's call this role the Host.

The Host can be a major contributor to your event in many ways. It is a crucial role.

So, what abilities should you look for in selecting your Host?

Here are some particular qualities that we have identified – some are more obvious than others;

- The Host needs to enjoy talking in an engaging way to camera, while at the same time remaining aware of everything that is going on in the event that is taking place around them.
- They must like people!
- They must speak clearly, eloquently and engagingly.
- They must come across as a warm and friendly personality in the gaze of the cold camera lens.
- They need to be able to remain absolutely calm and self-assured under pressure.
- They must have the intelligence to ask questions in interviews that will interest remote delegates.
- They need the journalistic ability to grasp the subject quickly and if necessary do the research they need to be a credible commentator. Armed with this knowledge, they should be capable of influencing your programme for the better.
- They need to have the ability of keeping to time, so the programme progresses on schedule.

In addition to all this, and probably the most vital quality of all to look for, is the ability to "fill". In other words, they know how to keep talking in an engaging way if things are not quite going according to plan!

The value of a good online Host in contributing to a successful event cannot be underestimated. It is a very worthwhile investment to take the time and trouble to find the right one.

The Host provides commentary, updates and reminders for your remote audience and can become a vital part of your event's construction. They will become the link, the conduit for your remote delegates. They are the voice of, dedicated to and represent the needs and interests of the remote audience. They will add a dimension that will be keep your remote attendees informed and engaged with all that is happening at your event as well as conducting interviews with 'thought leaders', speakers or delegates. These can be conducted at the back of the conference hall or, if there is one available, on a balcony overlooking the stage. On occasions we have set up a mini TV studio in a high footfall area, such as an exhibition or catering area, from which to provide this additional content. This has the added value of creating a bit of a buzz as near delegates gather round to see and hear what is going on. It's actually another great way of bringing your near and remote delegates together and reminding them of each other's existence.

Some other ways in which the Host can be used is to introduce pre-recorded video content and to manage dedicated Q&A sessions for the remote audience.

11. Interviewing

If you do decide to hold interviews with speakers after their presentations, or indeed with other commentators such as leading lights in your sector or simply passing delegates, there are a few things you can do to ensure success.

- Make sure that the interviewee knows what is expected of them before you start. Be clear on your timings and the objectives of the interview. Is this a 30 second vox pop or an in depth technical discussion? Is it to have some fun, ask some challenging questions provoked by the session, or talk about their latest book? The range of subjects and approaches is vast, so keep the focus on a particular area and brief the interviewer to keep things succinct and pithy.

- If the interviewee is one of your speakers after they have been on stage, then make sure they are prepared for this and know where to go after their presentation.

- Interviews have to be prepared, even if they are deemed to be a light hearted or fun conversation. Just because it's informal doesn't mean you can waste your remote delegates time with meaningless waffle.

- Make sure the interviewer knows that he or she is there to help the interviewee make a good impression and communicate points that the viewers are likely to find interesting and of value. They are not there to do a "Paxman" on the interviewee! It's worth bearing in mind that just because an interviewee is expert in their subject, that doesn't mean they will naturally be good in a general interview situation. This is where all the pre-production planning becomes so important and an interviewer with good technique earns their keep.

- From a logistical standpoint, chose your location carefully. You don't want to have to conduct the interview in hushed voices if another session is going on nearby. Neither do you want a PA system booming out public announcements and disturbing the interview. If you are in an area where there is a lot of activity and noise in the background, consider orientating the interview so that you can turn the camera towards the source of the hubbub and see it in the background behind the interview. "Noises off", for which the viewer can see the source are much less distracting and disturbing than unexplained noise.

While we are on the subject of noise, watch out for background music. You are very unlikely to have the rights to broadcast this music and may be infringing copyright if you do. That is one thing, but a more immediate problem you will have, if you are using YouTube Live Streaming, is that the stream may be cut by YouTube's highly sophisticated Digital Rights Management software!

- Standing or sitting? Think about furniture. Not just the colour and style, but the type of seating used or whether you need it at all. Standing interviews can work well, but only if they are very short. In depth discussions need to be conducted sitting down, but are high stools or easy chairs more appropriate? There is a tendency for people to slump back if the seating is too comfortable, whereas by and large you want the interviewees to be leaning forward and engaged. Avoid swivel chairs at all costs as people are prone to fidgeting, which can be very distracting for the viewer. Where will your Host put their notes and glass of water? You will most likely need some form of small table for this, but be careful of highly reflective glass and metal which may cause reflection problems for the camera.

- While technically and from the budget standpoint this may be no BBC Outside Broadcast, ensure you have adequate crew, video, sound and lighting equipment to do a good job. If you are live streaming the interviews, consider the logistics of achieving a good reliable internet connection at your chosen location.

- Deciding on the outcome of your interviews is as critical as the outcome of the conference sessions themselves. If you just throw an ill-considered interview in, for the sake of filling in time for the remote delegates, they will not thank you and you are likely to lose the audience. You need to inform and involve the interviewer in this process; let them know about the required outcomes and then let them work their magic for you.

12. Hub events

Hub, or if you prefer, satellite events create extra engagement.

Many associations have a geographically widespread membership. This may be across one nation or several countries or even continents. This is where hub events are much appreciated by members, allowing them to participate face to face, without the need to travel great distances.

As explained earlier, a hub event is effectively a breakout or mini conference remote from the main event. This allows delegates to gather together for a shared experience at a location that is easier to reach than the main conference location. Often they will join together to participate in the live streamed sessions. During meal and refreshment breaks, each hub event allows participants to network, discuss and explore issues raised during the sessions, in the same way as that afforded the *near audience* in the main conference centre.

To give you an example of the capability of hub events to dramatically extend the reach of your association's events, here are some statistics from a recent basic training course, run in Montreal, by The International Society for Ultrasound in Obstetrics and Gynaecology (ISUOG). They multiplied the size of their near audience in Montreal by more than eight times!

Near (on site) delegates	82	Total hub delegates	665
Hub / satellite events	23	Number of countries staging	14
Largest hub by delegates	72	Smallest hub by delegates	9

We've seen hub events have their own lunchtime speaker relevant to their specific region or complete standalone sessions. If you have multiple hubs taking place, consider having them carry out round table discussions or workshop groups following which the hubs report back to the main conference either through written documents or via an audio or video link.

The way hubs interact with the main event can be as simple or as complex as you wish, but always reference these activities back to your core objectives for the event to ensure that the hubs are supporting your overall aspirations.

13. Maximising the value of on demand

Most of this book is directed at generating remote engagement for live events. But a by-product of this activity is that you will be generating valuable recorded content, which can have a vital part to play in growing the value of your association to your members.

The fact is that some organisations choose not to live stream at all, but decide to capture the content purely for on demand access. Others, particularly those running multi room congresses, are likely to live stream selected high profile sessions while the remainder are recorded for post event viewing. In this context, typically, the lion's share of video consumed is on demand rather than live. So the importance of the on demand recordings should not be underestimated, and for educational content this is likely to be where you will get the most return on your investment.

On demand enables your audience to view the content to their schedule rather than one imposed upon them.

The recorded content can be edited and embedded into blog posts and news pages, transcribed for articles and books, incorporated in e-learning platforms or you can create an ever growing library of resources that will help to establish and maintain the position of your association as the first place to go for information and learning in your subject.

You can develop a marketing schedule using the content to keep the conversation going between your events and use selected clips to promote future events. If you have sponsors, they will love this as it offers further exposure for them. Members and non-members alike, that didn't attend your event will be able to have a sense of what happened and be encouraged to get involved next time.

There are endless opportunities to use this rich content to build the value offered to members and promote your association to non-members.

14. Evaluation

At the beginning of this book I looked at the importance of making the right strategic decisions for your association. I then went on to describe some practical and creative techniques to enable you to engage effectively with your remote delegates both live and on demand.

So what happens next?

After the event has concluded, you need to make sense of what has happened so that you can improve your future projects. In the first chapter, I said;

"Without a clear set of desired outcomes it's not surprising that results are likely to disappoint."

That is because, you need to know what you were aiming to achieve otherwise how on earth will you know if you've succeeded or failed? You need to have some set parameters by which to gauge your performance.

So let's assume that you took my advice and have a clear set of measurable and realistic objectives for this particular event. Your event has now come to an end and now is the time to review exactly what happened. This will enable you to make further strategic decisions that will specifically improve your future events and more generally help the positive development of your association.

Of course if you have been selling access to remote delegates you will already have the financial information from the payments process and know how you have performed in hard cash terms, but this gives no indication as to delegate satisfaction post event.

Evaluation is a procedure that is often overlooked or is simply not given enough thought. There are three main sources of data when it comes to measuring success with a remote audience.

1. Delegate surveys
2. Viewing statistics generated from the viewing pages and/or streaming server
3. Social media

Not carrying out a well-considered remote delegate survey is a significant missed opportunity! An effective delegate survey is the most informative and affordable way to gather meaningful and granular feedback as to how delegates value what you have provided. It also allows them to make observations and recommendations that should enable you to respond to their ongoing needs and develop your association to become an ever more effective and valuable resource.

In many ways this post-event research is as vital as meticulous pre-event planning and organisation. All too often we see the complete lack of a feedback loop, or worse still, if some kind of post event survey is carried out, the results are disregarded because the association leadership team are just not interested and want to move on to the next event. There can be a feeling of complacency that pervades after what seems (on the surface at least) to have been a successful event.

This is a sure route to stagnation and decline. The best associations are constantly talking to their members and surveys can form a vital component in this communication and development process.

Give time and effort to devising a *delegate survey* to elicit responses that will provide a genuine insight into what your delegates are thinking and then devote equivalent resources to analysing the results.

In contrast to the emotional and intellectual data that can be garnered from survey results, *viewing statistics*, provide a relatively easy and fast way to extract hard data about your event.

Exactly what information you can get will depend partly on the streaming service you use, as the quality and amount of data varies greatly.

By way of example, YouTube Live Streaming generates a spreadsheet report providing information as set out in the table below. This is typical of the kind of data you will get from the streaming server.

Video IDs:	*The unique YouTube identifier for you stream*
Start time:	*The time you started your live stream*
End time:	*The time you ended your live stream*
Playbacks	*The number of times the player has been activated*

Peak concurrent viewers	The highest number of viewers achieved at any one time
Total viewing time (hours)	*How many hours of video were watched*
Average session length (minutes)	*The average time that people watched in one sitting*
Country code	*A two letter code that denotes in which country viewers are located*
Playbacks	*The number of times the player is activated by a viewer in this country*
Peak concurrent viewers	*The highest number of viewers achieved in this country at any one time*
Total viewing time (hours)	*How many hours of video were watched in this country*
Average session length (minutes)	*The average time that people watched in one sitting in this country*

Another factor determining what information about the viewer is collected, is the method by which people are granted access to the viewing pages. Clearly an event where delegates are forced to register and log-in to participate will result in more data being generated than an open-to-all viewing page.

Often, viewing information from these various sources can provide a live snapshot of how your audience is building as your event progresses. If you monitor how things are going in real time, then you have the opportunity to do something about it if the remote audience numbers are lower than anticipated. For example, you may decide that you need to give an extra boost to your social media activity in order to try and build your audience.

Of course raw statistics alone, do not provide detailed insights into how much your viewers have taken on board or learnt, whether or not they enjoyed the experience, whether behaviours will change or if they value the event enough to decide to join a future event. This is where an online survey is indispensable.

There is a great deal of science and art in creating a survey that really works and there are many experts in the field with whom you can consult. If you are doing it yourself, I recommend applying three basic principles that I have found help to ensure you get a good response.

1. Be straightforward
    a. Keep the questions simple.
        It's all too easy to over complicate matters. That doesn't mean patronising your responders, but that you only tackle one concept per question.
    b. Use easily understood, plain language to avoid misinterpretation.
    c. Keep away from industry jargon and avoid acronyms that not everyone may understand or know.

2. Be positive

   a. Always try and phrase statements in the positive and be consistent in this. It is much more natural for respondents to "strongly agree" or score a higher number in response to a positive statement.

   For example, if you ask the respondents to rank their opinion on a scale from 'strongly disagree' to 'strongly agree', it works to make a statement you ask them to vote on such as;

   I learnt a great deal from the Professor's presentation

   Whereas it is confusing to state;

   I learnt nothing from the Professor's presentation

   And it's just as important to be consistent, as if you swap between positive and negative questions and statements, some people may miss the change and rank their answer at the opposite end of the scale to how they really feel.

3. Don't lead

   Avoid leading questions that push respondents towards your view of the correct answer. There is no right or wrong answer to questions of opinion, so beware of inadvertently imposing your views on others.

Combining your survey results data with viewing data from the streaming server and demographic information from registrations will provide you and your board with a good understanding of what worked and what didn't work and what and how you should change your event to be more effective next time around.

And don't forget to gather survey responses from *both* audiences, the near and remote. However, I recommend creating separate surveys for each. While many of the questions will be the same, it can become confusing as delegates will have experienced your event so differently.

And to form a complete picture of the success of your event, don't forget to take a good look at its impact on social media. If you don't already have this covered, there are many tools readily available such as Hootsuite[12], Tweetreach[13] and Sprout[14].

Bring all this data together and you should have a comprehensive measure of success to present to your association's board.

Have a good look at what worked and what didn't work. Think about what you would change and what you would like to do more / less of next time. If something didn't work, establish why. As you have it available, use the data rather than your instincts and relate the results to your original goals.

How the event has performed against those original objectives can help

---

[12] https://hootsuite.com/

[13] https://tweetreach.com/

[14] http://sproutsocial.com/

you decide your next steps in ever increasing engagement with your remote audience. This is vitally important as remote engagement is set to impact significantly on how associations develop and thrive.

15. In conclusion

Associations and other membership based organisations are confronted with an enormous opportunity to break out of the conference centre to reach new audiences.

Engaging with the hard to reach members who don't typically attend events is now attainable and affordable. The rapid advances in streaming technology and a general preparedness among audiences to engage online mean that webcasting of events is on the cusp of becoming mainstream.

This is only the beginning though, as new ideas and tools are emerging almost daily. With advances in 360-degree streaming and virtual reality (VR) the prospect for highly creative, immersive and engaging online events is extremely bright.

To be remotely engaging requires many of the same skills and techniques needed to successfully engage the audience in the room, but often with a twist.

I hope that in some small way this slim volume will help many conference organisers to figure out exactly how they need to twist their skills and techniques to remotely engage with these important audiences.

Remotely engaging events: –
some examples

I was very keen to include some good examples of remotely engaging events. But, rather than swamp you with a series of wordy, in-depth case studies, I have simply provided summaries of the relevant aspects of a range of projects.

The hope is that some of the techniques and approaches will spark off some ideas that you can use to extend the reach of your own events.

Event Camp Europe 2011

- Pushing the boundaries with event tech and lab rats.

- Took place in a Country House in Hertfordshire, England.

- 1 day only – full programme of speakers – mostly on location but some speakers came in remotely for special remote attendees viewing only, whilst the near delegates played croquet on the lawn!

- Event included 'Hub events' which took place in southern England, Sweden, Belgium and Poland.

- Full immersive hub experience as the Sweden hub led the Programme at the half way point of the day.

- Remote delegates took part from the USA, Canada and other parts of Europe.

- Event finished with a remotely engaging wine tasting between the hubs.

A key result of this event was to learn and demonstrate what could be done with some creative thinking and using the available technology to its fullest capability.

At the time of the event, Google Hangouts was very new, having been released just a few weeks earlier. We used Hangouts to enable delegates to see and hear the hub participants. Of course there were mistakes and glitches, from which we learned a great deal. This was a very innovative event for its time and some of the techniques used have since been incorporated by event organisers into other events.

Event Camp Oz 2012

- Conference that combined near and far delegates.
- Took place over 2 days.
- Held in Sydney Australia and all but two locally based speakers delivered their presentations remotely.
- One of the goals of the event was to achieve a Sustainability Certification.

A major objective of this event was to show that event organisers could deliver events that successfully mixed remote and live speakers.

The sustainability initiative demonstrated that it is no longer essential for event organisers to incur the financial and environmental cost of speakers flying thousands of miles across the globe to deliver a 30-minute presentation. At the time of this event, remote presentations were a rarity.

Event Camp Middle East at GIBTM 2014

The following is a blog post written a couple of months after the event, for Reed Exhibitions Knowledge Week.

> *Whenever event technology is being discussed, Hybrid Events are increasingly on the agenda. More often than not the discussion tends to revolve around attracting and keeping a remote audience, whether it should be free or paid for and ways to fund the activity in the first place. It is not often that the conversation moves onto the subject of remote presenters.*

> *The concept of being more sustainable as well as reducing travel budgets by allowing delegates to attend a conference online / virtually / remotely (use your preferred adjective) is now a generally accepted one. But organisers have the opportunity to go one step further and engage remote speakers to contribute to their event.*

> *This can significantly help an organiser's bottom line as well as allow access to key speakers who may otherwise be unavailable. It may be possible, for example, for a world expert in the subject of the conference to give an hour of their time to present from their home or workplace, whereas the demands and costs of flying across continents to speak in person may preclude their availability and/or affordability. Done correctly, this*

approach allows great scope for all delegates – in the room or in the cloud – to learn, engage and interact with the speaker wherever they are located.

It was to explore exactly this approach that, together with Paul Cook of PlanetPlanit.biz and supported by friends at ShowGizmo, we undertook Event Camp Middle East 2014. Held in Abu Dhabi, UAE, as part of Reed Exhibitions' GIBTM show in March. This particular Event Camp adopted a theme of sustainability; all speakers with the exception of one (who happened to be in the location anyway) and event host Paul Cook, presented from their home countries and were beamed into the room and out again to a dedicated event microsite.

The online event was created using YouTube Live Streaming and the remote speakers made their contribution via Skype. Promoted through Twitter and Facebook, Event Camp Middle East 2014 was a global hybrid conference, where the speakers were located in 7 different countries and attracted online delegates in 12 countries around the globe, as well as the audience 'in the room' at ADNEC in Abu Dhabi.

The 'virtual presenters' were located in Australia, New Zealand, Europe, the USA and Canada. Delegates, both in the room and online, were able to interact with comments and questions through an interactive panel on the web page alongside the video player. Event host Paul Cook as well as linking and introducing speakers also conducted interviews with many. The recordings were available through YouTube immediately afterwards and the event microsite was updated with the on demand recordings the next day. (One of the lesser known advantages of YouTube Live Streaming is that it has a DVR function. This is like a Sky+ or Tivo facility, where if a viewer joins a live webcast late they are able to watch it live or rewind back to earlier in the presentation.)

The stated aim of the Event Camp community is "to bring together like-minded professionals, to share best practices, and learn new strategies, for leveraging social media and technology to create enhanced event experiences." Event Camps are intended to push the boundaries of trying and testing new ideas, so using speakers contributing remotely fitted well with this ethos.

The sessions are available on demand[15] and continue to be widely viewed and commented upon.

---

[15] http://bit.ly/ecme14ondemand

Strong Voices 2015

Conference programme designed to provide project reports from an Arts Council funded initiative.

- Took place at the Sage in Newcastle
- 1 day only – concurrent sessions on the programme
- Main room was streamed live
- Interviews with speakers and thought leaders were streamed live between conference sessions
- Programme design enabled remote delegates to be fully involved in asking questions, voting and taking part in group exercises.

(Produced in association with Becki Cross, Events Northern.)

As accessibility for all was a fundamental principle of this Arts Programme, it was imperative that anyone attending the event was able to participate fully.

This resulted in careful event design, to make sure that remote delegates could contribute as fully as delegates in the room.

BSL signers were deployed through the whole day for the benefit of both near and remote audiences.

National Speakers Association 2015

A training session which was part of the NSA Conference Programme.

- Took place in southern England and Washington, USA.
- Software video conference set up allowed synchronised audio and video dialogue between two co-presenters – one in each location.
- Content involved the two speakers presenting their thoughts and experiences to other professional speakers in the conference room in Washington on the skills and practicalities of remote speaking.
- What better way of demonstrating this than actually doing it live.

As the two presenters were thousands of miles apart, this training session proved that they didn't need to be in the same room for the delegates (other professional speakers) to gain real benefit. In fact a number of the delegates actually forgot the separation, because of how immersive the session was.

The big advantage of this approach to live remote training was that the delegates were able to see behind the scenes. They could see the detail that needs to go into making a remote session work for delegates.

Sedex Global Responsible Sourcing Conferences 2012 - 2016

Since 2012, we have web broadcast the annual conference for Sedex, a day of cutting edge debate and discussions.

Sedex, the Supplier Ethical Data Exchange, is a not for profit membership organisation dedicated to driving improvements in responsible and ethical business practices in global supply chains. With members in 150 countries, Sedex are keen to make it possible for ALL members to have the opportunity to get involved in the annual conference.

Key objectives are:

- Engage with wider membership unable to attend physically
- Build the profile of the association year round
- Show thought leadership by leading debates on vital topics
- Build an educational resource for members
- The live webcast and on demand recordings are free to all, though people are required to register for the live webcast, and provide basic credentials. This policy was adopted in order to enable members unable to travel to London to join in and benefit from the event. Sedex are also keen to engage with non-members and stakeholders without any barriers.
- The online event was shortlisted for Best Event Webcasting at the International and European Association Awards 2015.

Data from the last three years of the Sedex Global Responsible Sourcing Conference is shown in the charts below, demonstrating how this association has increasingly engaged with their remote audience.

Sedex, the Supplier Ethical Data Exchange, Annual Conference 2014, 2015, 2016
A story of increasing remote engagement

The International Society for Ultrasound in Obstetrics and Gynaecology (ISUOG)

ISUOG have a regular programme of training events that are streamed live and on-demand, enabling medical professionals the world over to benefit from the education they provide.

With the emergence of the Zika virus, they decided that an outreach webcast was needed to allow members and non-members alike to learn about the latest diagnostic techniques.

It was decided that to engage the most people, the webcast needed to be in three languages (English, Portuguese and Spanish) and should take place twice to cater for key time zones. Effectively 6 separate 90 minute webcasts.

For consistency it was decided to pre-record the lectures – which lasted around an hour – and conclude with a 30-minute-long, live Q&A chat session to enable delegates to respond to what they had heard and learnt and to investigate further.

The two webcasts were highly successful as the following stats indicate.

- 2648 viewers in total
- Viewers in 74 countries
- 605 comments made / questions asked

.

About the authors

Martin Shepherdly left Art College with qualifications in graphics and advertising. His early working years were spent creating and producing large scale conferences and product launches for major global brands like Kellogg's, IBM, Mercedes-Benz and BT.

Martin has always been driven by a constant desire to find innovative ways to communicate and engage with audiences. In May 2005, just two weeks before YouTube launched, he moved into the streaming video market, anticipating its rapid growth and the opportunities it presented to reach global audiences. His vision was shared by a long term industry colleague, Mark Buckland, and in 2008 the two came together to form BeThere Global, a company that uses sophisticated recording and streaming technology to help clients unlock the full value of their congress, conference or seminar.

BeThere Global is now a leading provider of recording and web streaming services to the conference and events industry and with an extensive client list covering the commercial, public, medical and association sectors.

With his extensive track record in face-to-face events coupled with in depth knowledge and experience of virtual and hybrid events Martin is a uniquely qualified consultant for organisations developing a strategy for expanding the reach and impact of their events.

Paul Cook found his way into the world of events by working in insurance and risk management. It was whilst he was at Pinewood Studios that he began a deeper understanding of how films and productions are created. Watching scenes being constructed and then edited in post-production gave Paul some fascinating insights. He uses this knowledge and applies it to the events he designs and produces.

Paul has been a remote speaker, a remote host, a live host, a co-producer and producer of numerous events that combine the two sets of delegates. He is a strong believer in the value of content at events and strives to engage delegates for an immersive experience.

One client sums up Paul's work in this way – "I've worked with Paul for the past two years and what I like about him is the fresh approach he takes to designing, planning and executing new forms of events and meetings. He is currently among the small group of global leaders who are changing the way we meet and share information, and his advocacy of the hybrid event, together with his expert knowledge on the subject, means that we will all be meeting in very different ways".

Paul has extensive experience of membership associations and is of the opinion that 'remotely engaging events' will be required by many organisations to enhance their member value and grow the association.

Get in touch

Martin Shepherdly

martin@bethereglobal.com

🐦 @bethereglobal

Paul Cook

paul@planetplanit.biz

🐦 @planetplanitbiz

Manufactured by Amazon.ca
Bolton, ON

11979635R00061